Bulletin Boards That Teach

Joy Evans & JoEllen Moore

Contents

Lift each little turtle's shell
To see if you have answered well

Reproduce the turtle pattern on pages 3 and 4. If you take this pattern to an instant copy shop, they can run it on colored card stock that is sturdy and attractive. Run five copies of each pattern.

One sheet is Turtle's top.

One sheet is a backing paper and Turtle's legs.

Cut out the patterns.

Insert a paper clip in the backing paper to hold the answer to the problem. Then you can easily change cards.

Staple the shell over the backing sheet.

Pin in place on the bulletin board.

Speech Bubbles

Cut out scalloped white speech bubbles.

Insert a paper clip to hold the problem to be solved. Pin them on the board.

This makes it easy to switch problems when children have mastered the first set.

Caption

Print the couplet on SHELF PAPER with felt pen.

Bulletin Boards That Teach

Turtle Bulletin Board

Use this board for daily practice in solving word problems. Do one problem orally each day. Change problems weekly.

- This bulletin board may also be used as a self-checking center activity.
- Write problems and answers on cards. Be sure they are large enough to see at a distance.

Sample Problems and Answers:

Tillie Turtle had 9 baby turtles. Myrtle Turtle had 16 baby turtles. How many more babies did Myrtle have than Tillie?	16 babies −9 babies ———— 7 babies
Turtle A weighs 4 pounds. Turtle B weighs 7 pounds. Turtle C weighs 2 pounds. Which turtle is heaviest? Which turtle is lightest?	Turtle B is heaviest. Turtle C is lightest.
I went 2 feet down the path, 4 feet over a rock, and 3 feet across the grass. How far did I go?	2 feet 4 feet +3 feet ———— 9 feet
8 turtles went on a picnic. Half were boy turtles. Half were girl turtles. How many were girls? How many were boys?	4 girls 4 boys
If one turtle cost 20¢, how much would 3 turtles cost?	20¢ 20¢ +20¢ ———— 60¢
Tammi saw 56 flies. She ate 29 flies. How many flies got away from Tammi?	56 flies −29 flies ———— 27 flies got away
Teddy left home at 8:00. It took him 3 hours to get to the library. What time was it when Teddy got there?	8:00 1 9:00 2 10:00 3 11:00 11:00
I spent 23¢ for a bag of food. I gave the clerk a quarter. How much change did I get back?	25¢ −23¢ ———— 2¢ change
Take a ruler. Measure my shell. How tall is it? How wide is it?	6½ 7
There were 378 eggs laid in the sand. Each mother turtle laid the same number of eggs. If there were 9 mother turtles, how many eggs did each lay?	42 eggs 9)378 36 —— 18 18

Turtle Pattern for Problem Solving Bulletin Board

Turtle Pattern for Problem Solving Bulletin Board

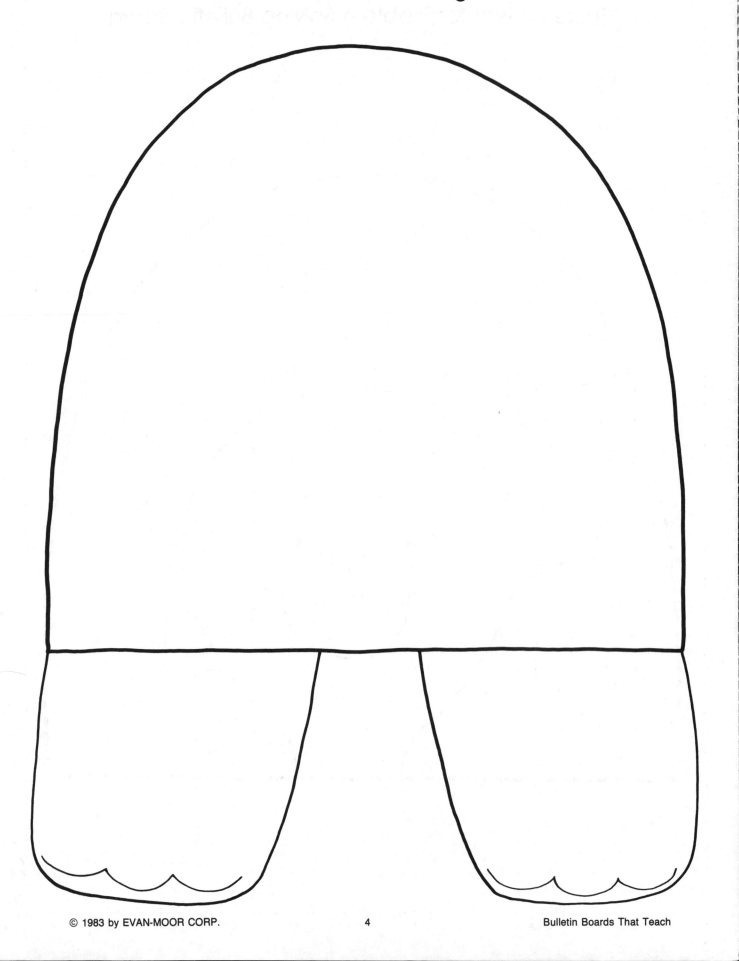

4   Bulletin Boards That Teach

Catch my mistake!

Baseball Player

Use pattern page 8 for our baseball player's head. Use felt pens or crayons to add color and contrast.

Pin up a REAL baseball hat to give that three-dimensional look.

Slip head inside

Make his body from a piece of construction paper. Round the top corners.

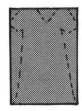 

Add a number to his jersey?

Ball and Mitt

Cut out and color the pattern on page 7.

Cut a rectangle for an arm.

Pin arm and glove together.

Speech Bubble

Cut a speech bubble from white paper.

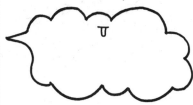

Insert a paper clip. Slip a new card in each day to drill punctuation skills.

     Bulletin Boards That Teach

Baseball Bulletin Board

Use this bulletin board for daily practice in capitalization and punctuation.

- Write the sentences to be punctuated large enough to be seen at a distance. Change the sentences daily.

- Select children to locate and correct errors using marking pens. With young children, you may prefer to make the corrections as children give the answers.

Sample sentences:

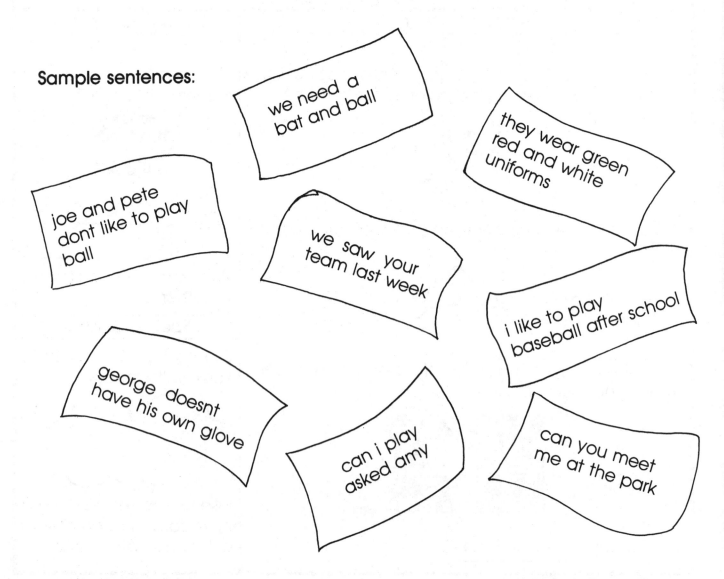

we need a bat and ball

they wear green red and white uniforms

joe and pete dont like to play ball

we saw your team last week

i like to play baseball after school

george doesnt have his own glove

can i play asked amy

can you meet me at the park

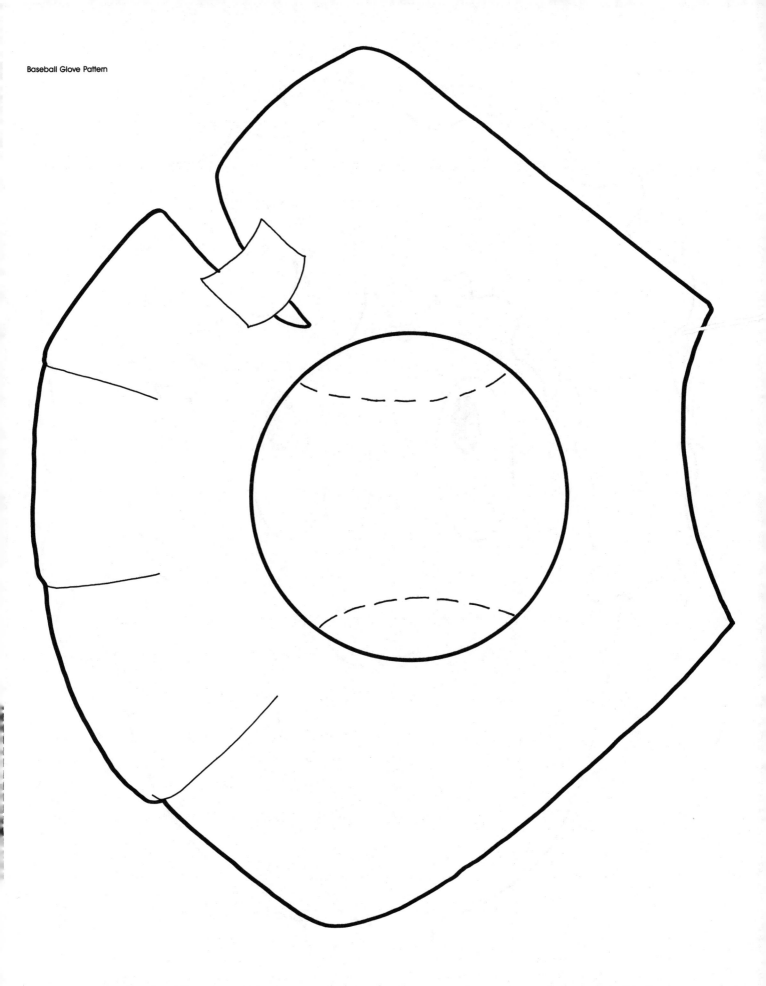

7

8 Bulletin Boards That Teach

Time

Our clock has –

2 hands –
    1 hour hand
    1 minute hand

2 halves of
30 minutes each

12 numbers
for 12 hours

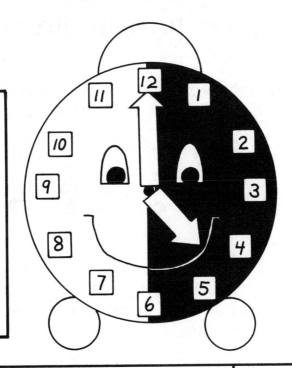

flashcards

The Clock

You need–felt, heavyweight Pellon, paper, and a thumbtack. The clock face is made of 2 FELT half-circles. Cut from two different colors of felt to emphasize concept of half-hours.
Pin on bulletin board. Put a THUMBTACK to mark the center.

Use the Pellon to make the rest of the clock parts. You can print directly on the Pellon and then cut out the shapes you need.

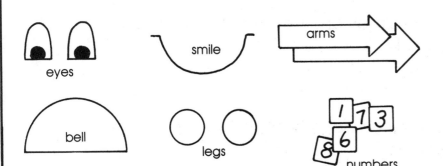

eyes

smile

arms

bell

legs

numbers

Now you have a clock you can put together with the students. It can also serve as a center activity that provides practice in time-telling principles.

The Chart

List the basic concepts about the clock or telling time that you want students to be aware of.

Flashcards

Make available flash-cards (page 11) which can be utilized in a quick daily review or as a part of a center. They should be self-checking.

Time Bulletin Board

Use this board for daily practice in telling time. The felt face and Pellon hands and numbers work in the same manner as a flannel board.

- Remove numbers. Pass them out to various children. They must put them back around the clock face in the correct order.

- Each day select 2 or 3 flashcards from the pocket. Select children to take a card and place the Pellon hands in the correct position. Begin with hours and work up to 5 minutes.

- Have a child move the hands of the clock to a time _____ hours and minutes earlier or later than the time shown on the clock face.

- This bulletin board may also be used as a selfchecking center activity.

- Use the worksheet on page 12 in class or send home for extra practice.

3:00		**9:00**	
11:00		**2:30**	
4:30		**9:30**	
6:30		**5:15**	
7:05		**1:25**	
10:45		**8:10**	

Make Your Own Clock

You need: this paper, scissors, a paper fastener and a brain ready to go to work.

1. Add numbers.
2. Cut out.
3. Fasten on arms.
4. Practice with your clock.

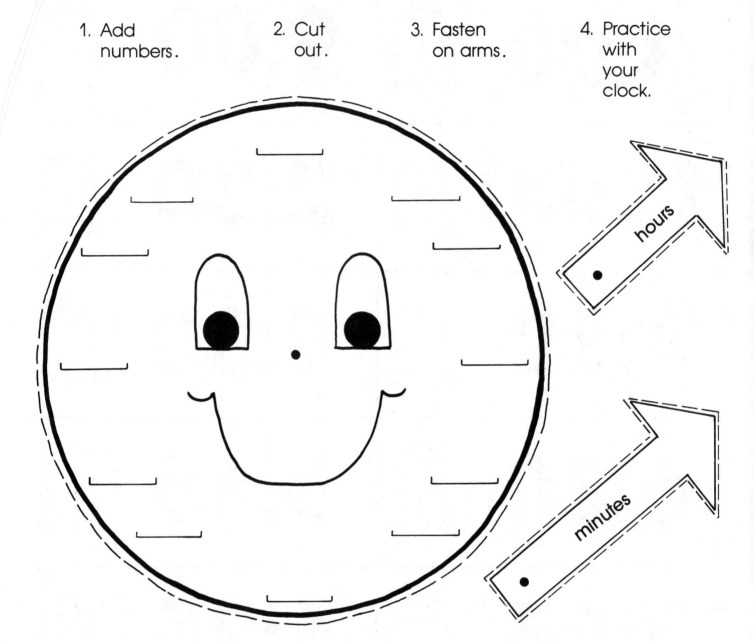

PRACTICE: Check off the ones you know.		
5:00 ✓	2:30	5:15
7:05	9:00	4:30
6:30	8:05	2:05
10:45	1:30	3:00

Bulletin Boards That Teach

Shop here.
Pick three.
Add them up.
Pay for them.

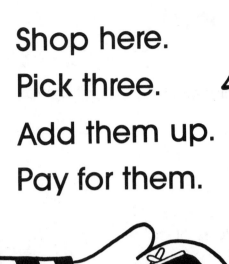

Store

Reminder		
penny	=	1¢
nickel	=	5¢
dime	=	10¢
quarter	=	25¢
half dollar	=	50¢
dollar	=	100¢
		or $1.00

The Hand

Cut the hand from flesh colored construction paper. Cut 2 pieces at the same time.

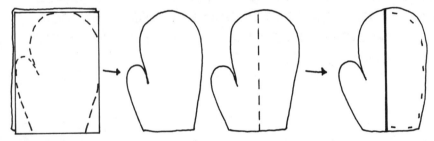

Slice one piece down the center. Staple to the hand so you have a pocket to put a coin purse in.
Place a new amount of change in the purse each day.
Real coins are preferable.

The arm is a rectangle with stripes.

You may use fabric here for an interesting effect.

Make a pocket to hold receipts. See page 15.	Display the Reminder chart on page 16.	**Note** Laminating all items on this board is a good idea.

Store

Use large tag and create a rectangle with two pockets—.

Add a roof.

Staple on.

Have children cut pictures of desirable objects from magazines and paste to construction paper. You price them before placing them in the store pockets.

Pin up a small box to hold change.

Money Bulletin Board

Use this board for daily practice in recognizing coins and in computing values of money.

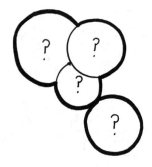

- Review the names and values of coins daily.

- Select one child to count the money in the coin purse. A second child selects a picture from the "store." The class must decide if there is enough money to buy the item and the amount of change left. You may continue by selecting two other items and using the "receipt" on page 15.

- Change the sums of money daily.

- This bulletin board becomes an activity center by using the "store" and the receipt form.

receipt

I have _____ ¢.

I spent _____ ¢

_____ ¢

_____ ¢

Total _____

Now I will see if I get change.

I had _____ ¢

I spent _____ ¢

What is left? _____ ¢

Do you get change back? _____

receipt

I have _____ ¢.

I spent _____ ¢

_____ ¢

_____ ¢

Total _____

Now I will see if I get change.

I had _____ ¢

I spent _____ ¢

What is left? _____ ¢

Do you get change back? _____

Reminder

penny	=	1¢
nickel	=	5¢
dime	=	10¢
quarter	=	25¢
half dollar	=	50¢
dollar	=	100¢ or $1.00

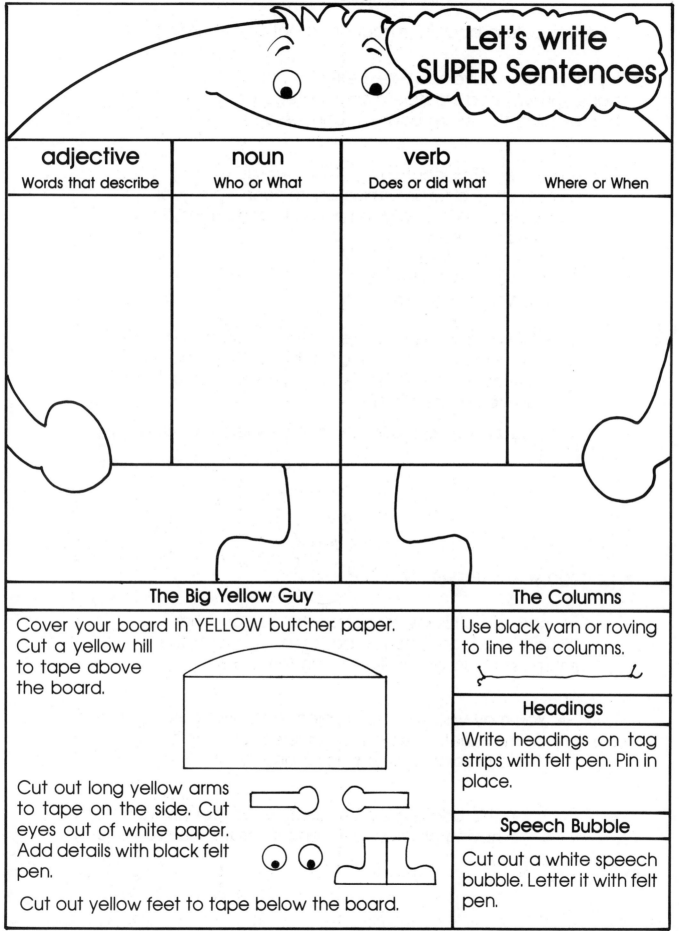

Let's write SUPER Sentences

adjective	noun	verb	
Words that describe	Who or What	Does or did what	Where or When

The Big Yellow Guy

Cover your board in YELLOW butcher paper. Cut a yellow hill to tape above the board.

Cut out long yellow arms to tape on the side. Cut eyes out of white paper. Add details with black felt pen.

Cut out yellow feet to tape below the board.

The Columns

Use black yarn or roving to line the columns.

Headings

Write headings on tag strips with felt pen. Pin in place.

Speech Bubble

Cut out a white speech bubble. Letter it with felt pen.

17

Sentence Bulletin Board

Use this bulletin board for frequent practice in building sentences.

- If your students have had no experience with sentence parts, you will need practice in each category of words before using the entire board in one lesson.

    - Pass out cards containing single words or simple phrases. Have class determine where each word goes. You will find sample cards on pages 19 and pages 20.
        #1 Name Words
        #2 Action Words
        #3 Words that describe
        #4 Where or when

        Children may build simple sentences after #1 and #2 are on the board. More complicated sentences are developed as #3 and #4 are added. Children may add determiners orally.

        fuzzy   caterpillar   munches leaves   all day

        "A fuzzy caterpillar munches leaves all day."

- Change words frequently.

    - For more practice, write out sentences and have children read and name parts as you cut the sentences apart and put them on the board.

        - You may wish to place subject and predicate signs on the bulletin board. Place subject over parts 1 and 2 and predicate over parts 3 and 4.

            - This board may be used as an activity center by having children write and illustrate their sentences.

18   Bulletin Boards That Teach

fluffy

duck

yellow

snake

slippery

guppie

happy

kitten

swam

outside

slept

all day

hurried

by the tree

played

in the pond

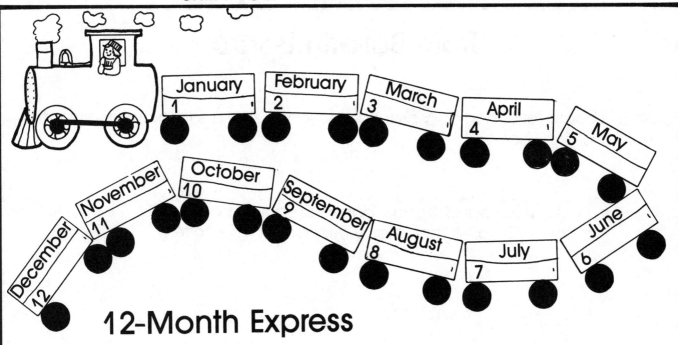

12-Month Express

Engine	Cars
Reproduce the engine pattern on page 23. Color it with felt pens in bright colors.	Fold construction paper to form pockets.

Use cotton to create three-dimensional smoke puffs rising from the smoke stack.

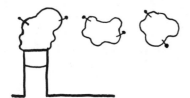

Pin it in place wherever it fits.

Allow room across your board or above the board to pin up the twelve cars that hold the names of the months.

Use many colors. Staple.

Cut black round wheels. Paste to the cars.

Number the cars with felt pen.

Flashcards

Print the names of the months on cards. Place in pockets in order.

May

Train Bulletin Board

Use this board for a short daily practice in recognizing and placing in order the months of the year.

- Pass out several of the flashcards containing names of months. Children then place the cards in the correct train car.

- Ask a riddle. Select a child to remove the card which gives the answer to the riddle.

Example:
When this month comes around, smart turkeys can't be found.
(November)

Fireworks flash in the summer sky, when it is the 4th of _____ .
(July)

- You may wish to cut the ends of the flashcards, so the pieces will fit together like a puzzle. Children can then use the board as a self-checking activity center.
    Example:

- Use the worksheet on page 24 as a class or homework assignment.

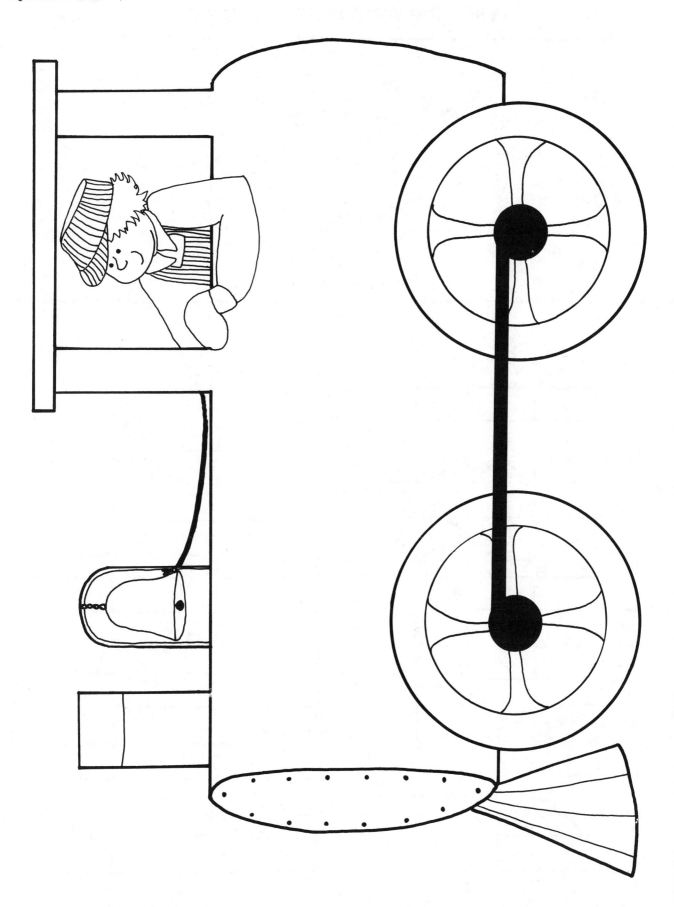

Write the months in the boxes.

August

October

March

February

June

January

November

May

December

April

September

July

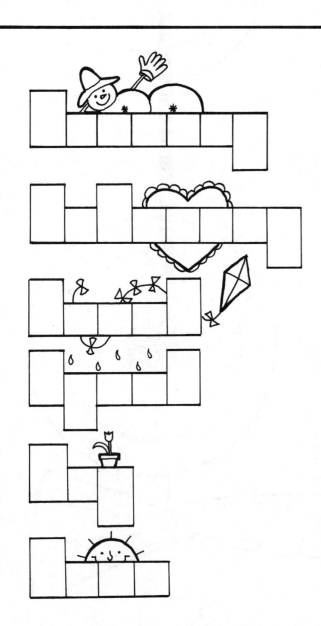

24

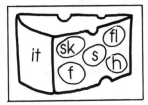

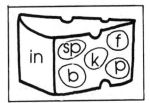

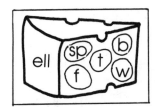

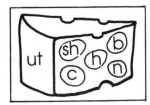

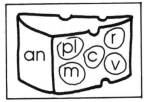

Mmmm

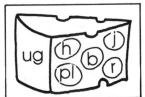

Mouse

Use pattern page 28 for the mouse. Color the mouse gray and give him a wonderfully pink nose.

Add a tail of black roving.

Cheese

Use the cheese pattern on page 27. Reproduce several of these pages so you can emphasize many word families. Use felt pen to add the word families you are using.

Mouse Bulletin Board

Use this board for daily practice in reading word families. It can also be used for identifying rhyming patterns.

- Take a few minutes each day to read several word families. Change the mouse's "cheese" weekly.

- Ask riddles to practice rhyming.
  "I make a ringing sound.
  I rhyme with fell."   (sound like)

- Give children copies of the "cheese" pattern on page 27. They may practice word families already covered or create their own.

Sample Word Families

_an	_it	_ug	_in	_ut	_ell	_atch
pan	bit	bug	bin	but	tell	catch
ran	fit	hug	fin	cut	fell	match
plan	hit	jug	pin	hut	bell	hatch
can	sit	rug	kin	nut	well	patch
man	pit	plug	spin	shut	shell	latch
van	flit	shrug	skin	strut	spell	snatch

_ake	_ay	_ow	_ow	_ong	_edge	_ink
bake	bay	low	cow	long	hedge	pink
cake	jay	snow	now	gong	ledge	wink
lake	clay	bow	how	song	wedge	rink
stake	stay	grow	plow	wrong	pledge	link
flake	play	show	bow	along	sledge	think
shake	away	elbow	brow	strong	dredge	drink

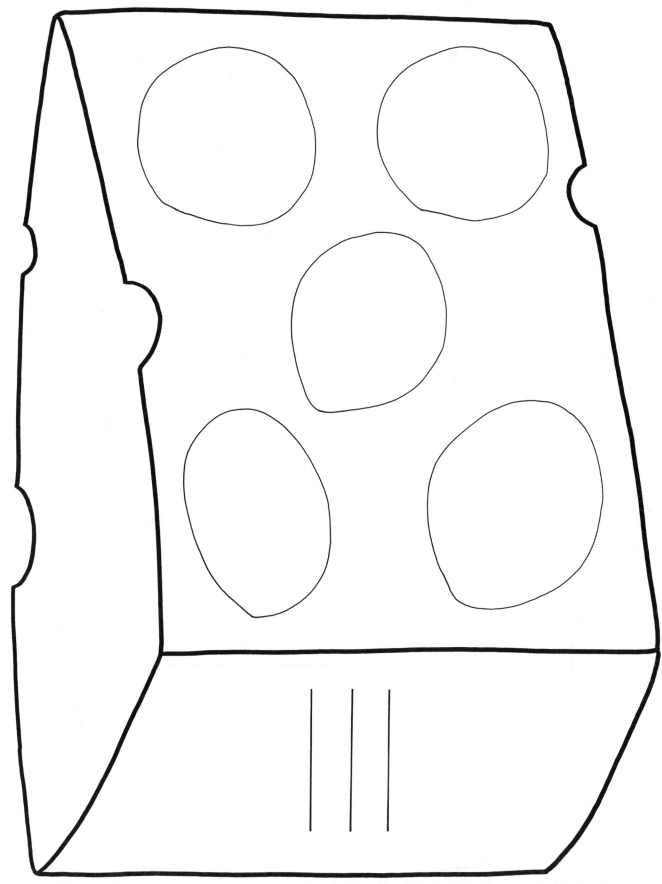

Mouse Pattern for Word Families Board

28

Shapes

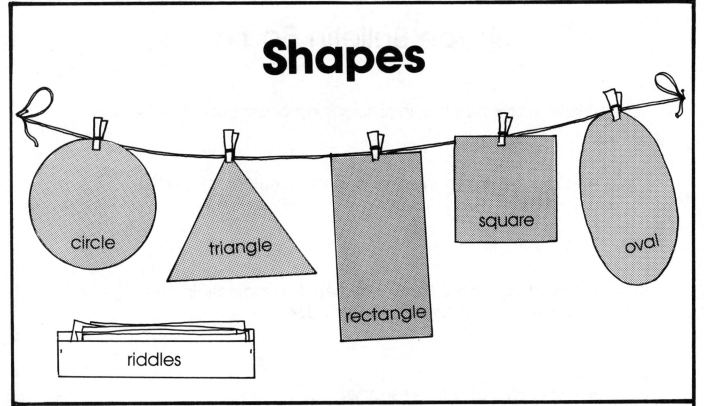

The Shapes

Cut all basic shapes from tagboard. Print shape names with felt pen and laminate to increase durability.

This board is one that can be used throughout the year in a primary classroom. Display it somewhere close at hand so you can "pluck" the shape you are reviewing at any given moment.

Tack up a length of rope   and hang your shapes with clothespins. It is extra useful if you hang it so that students can reach it too.

Make a construction paper pocket labeled "riddles." Write riddles about shapes on tag strips. See page 30.

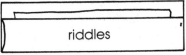

riddles

       Bulletin Boards That Teach

Shape Bulletin Board

Use this board for practice in recognizing basic geometric shapes.

- Introduce the names and characteristics of each shape.

- Select a shape. Have children find objects in the classroom that are the same shape.

- Ask riddles about the shapes.

> What shape has 3 corners
> and 3 sides?
> I am the shape of the full moon.
> Most doors and tables are my shape.
> I have no corners. I look like
> a squeezed circle.
> What shape has 4 corners and
> 4 sides of the same length?

- This board may be used as an activity center using the picture cards on page 31 and page 32. Provide envelopes containing shapes for children to use in reproducing the pictures shown.

   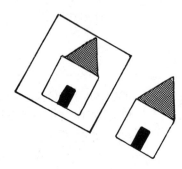

Shape Pictures—Reproduce, cut apart and paste on tag.

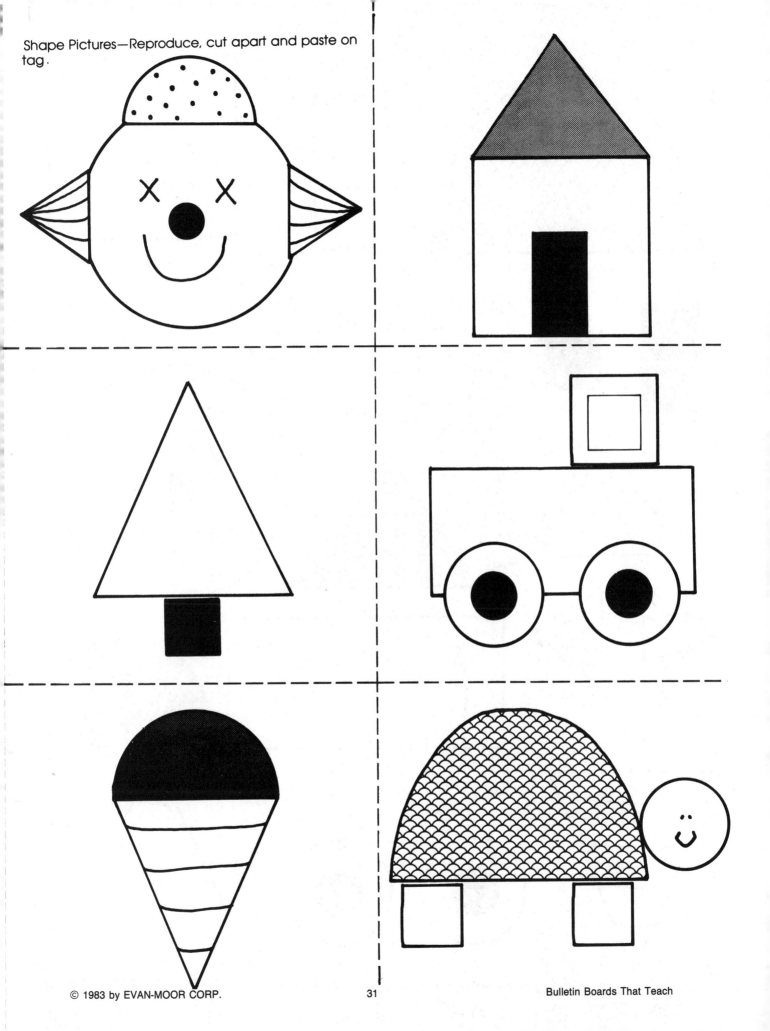

31

Shapes—Reproduce, cut out and paste on tag.

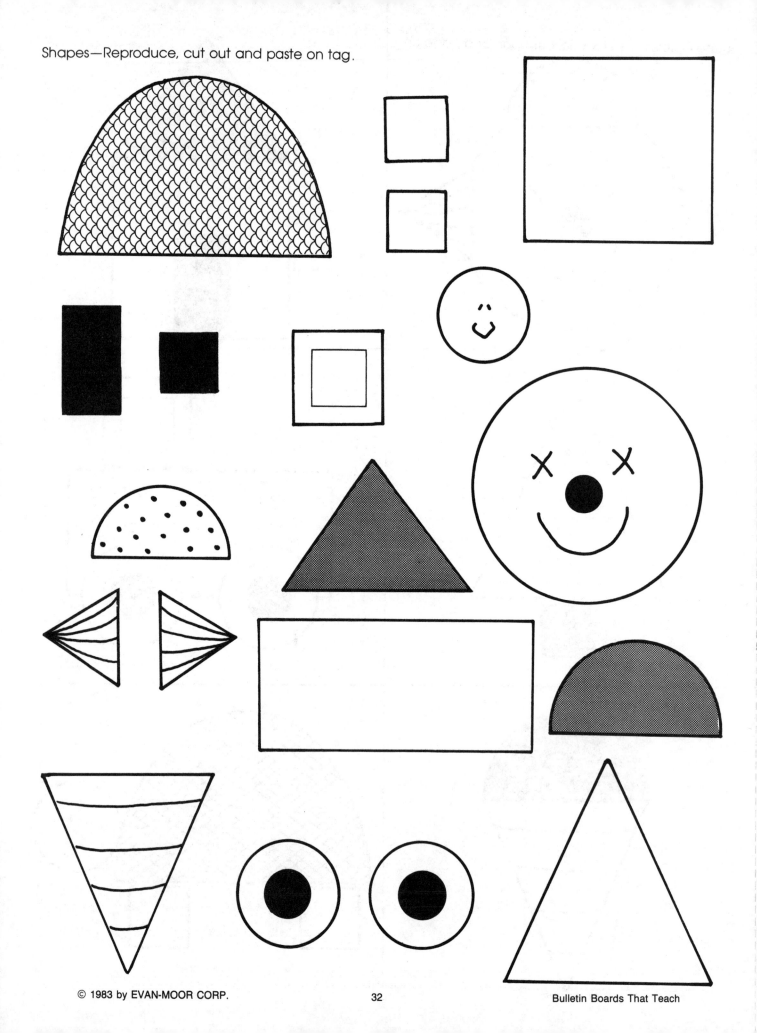

32

"The time has come," the walrus said, "to speak of many things!"

Tara said, "This lava rock is light."

"I loved the surprise," said Lou.

"You will like this book," said John.

The Walrus

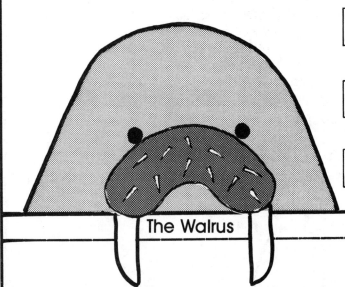

Cut a large piece of BROWN tag in a hill shape.

Cut a BLACK snout.

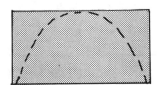

Paste toothpick pieces randomly.

Cut YELLOW tusks.

Paste all parts together. Add the eyes with black felt pen.

Pin at the lower end of board with tusks hanging over.

Caption

Cut off a long strip of white shelf paper.
Letter the caption with felt pen.

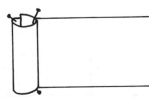

Quote Strips

Letter tag strips with felt pen.

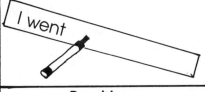

Backing

BLUE or YELLOW are good choices for background.

 Bulletin Boards That Teach

Walrus Bulletin Board

Use this board to practice the use of quotation marks.

- As children share information about themselves, hobbies, etc., add sentence strips to the bulletin board. This way the board changes daily or weekly.

Pete said, "I like to fish."

worms

"My baby sister can crawl," explained Ann.

- You may write the sentences without quotation marks, then select a child to come up and add punctuation.

- Use the worksheets on page 35 and 36 for class use, homework or in an activity center.

Name _____

Today in our class we had sharing. It was interesting. I learned that

1. _____

2. _____

3. _____

 Put in the quotation marks .

 Mother said, It is time for school.

 Come and get your dinner, Skipper, called Pete.

 May I have a piece of cake? asked Carlos

 Andy yelled, Jump into the water now.

 I can beat anyone in a race, bragged the hare.

 Catch the ball! shouted Margo.

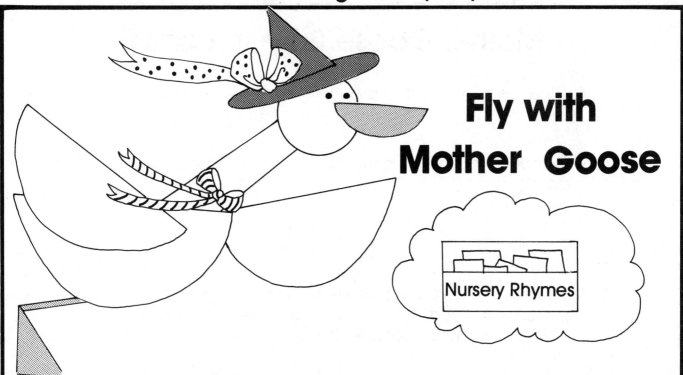

Fly with Mother Goose

Nursery Rhymes

Mother Goose	Backing

Mother Goose

Cut these basic shapes from construction paper. Cut them large enough to **fill** your board.

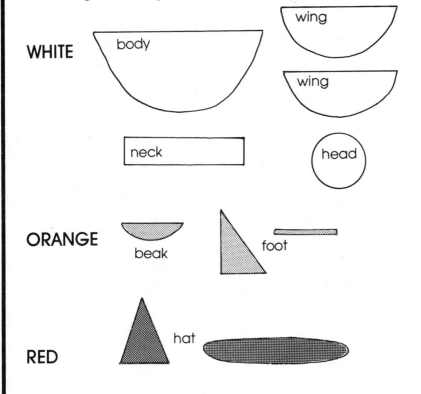

WHITE — body, wing, wing, neck, head

ORANGE — beak, foot

RED — hat

Use real ribbon to create a bow around her neck and on her hat.

Pin all parts in place on your board.

Backing

Use butcher paper to back your board.

BLUE

WHITE

Caption

Cut block letters from BLACK construction paper.

Nursery Rhyme Pocket

Make a pocket from WHITE construction paper.

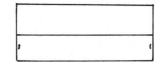

Fill it with nursery rhyme pictures on pages 39 and 40.

Mother Goose Bulletin Board

Use this bulletin board to practice recall of nursery rhymes.

- Introduce nursery rhymes to class over a period of days.

- Review one or more rhymes daily. A child selects a picture card from the pocket. Using the picture as a clue to the rhyme, child recites the verse.

- Child selects a card, then asks classmates a riddle about the picture. Class gives answer by reciting correct nursery rhyme.

"I jumped over a candlestick."

"I lost all my sheep."

"I eat curds and whey.
A spider scared me."

- Use the board as an activity center.

Picture Cards for Nursery Rhyme Bulletin Board

Dickory Dickory Dare

There Was An Old Woman

Humpty Dumpty

Jack Be Nimble

Wee Willie Winkie

Little Miss Muffet

© 1983 by EVAN-MOOR CORP.

Bulletin Boards That Teach

Peter Peter Pumpkin Eater

Pease Porridge

Hey Diddle Diddle

Mary Had A Little Lamb

Jack and Jill

Little Boy Blue

Bulletin Boards That Teach

Skill Area — **Sequencing**

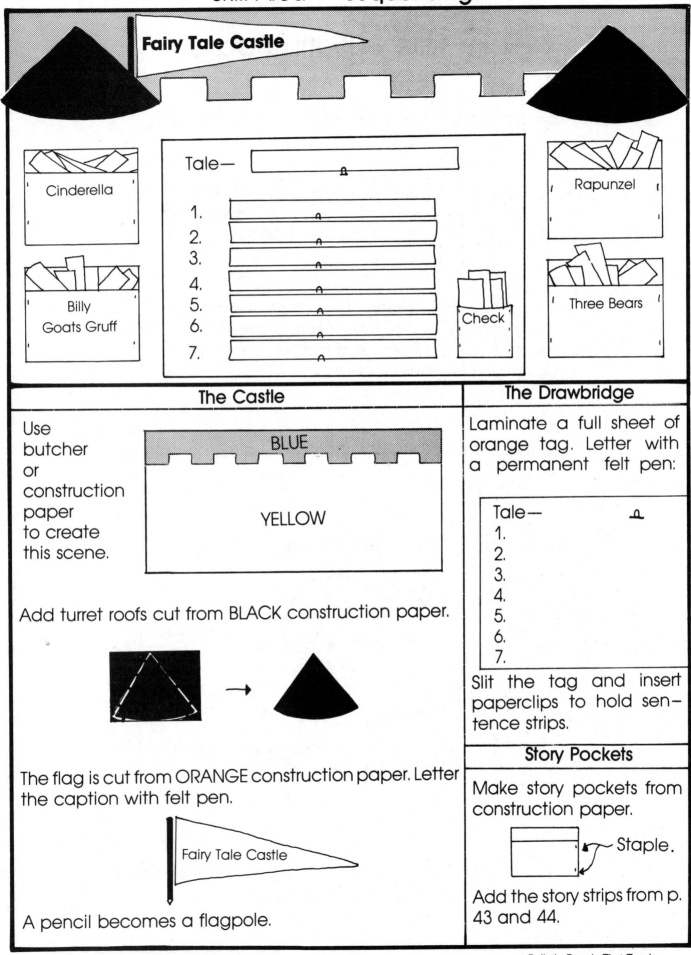

Fairy Tale Castle

Cinderella

Billy
Goats Gruff

Tale—

1.
2.
3.
4.
5.
6.
7.

Check

Rapunzel

Three Bears

The Castle

Use
butcher
or
construction
paper
to create
this scene.

BLUE

YELLOW

Add turret roofs cut from BLACK construction paper.

The flag is cut from ORANGE construction paper. Letter
the caption with felt pen.

Fairy Tale Castle

A pencil becomes a flagpole.

The Drawbridge

Laminate a full sheet of
orange tag. Letter with
a permanent felt pen:

Tale—
1.
2.
3.
4.
5.
6.
7.

Slit the tag and insert
paperclips to hold sen-
tence strips.

Story Pockets

Make story pockets from
construction paper.

Staple.

Add the story strips from p.
43 and 44.

Fairy Tale Bulletin Board

Use this board for frequent practice in sequencing.

- Be sure to use stories which are familiar to your students. You may wish to begin with fewer sentences, building up to 7 as the children become more skillful.

- Pass the cards out to students. Have the class decide the correct order. Place the cards on the castle board. The class should then read the sentences in order to double-check their accuracy.

- Change the stories as the class successfully completes each set.

- The board may be used as a center activity.

- You will find sentences for 2 stories on pages 43 and 44. Write each sentence on a tag strip.

Goldilocks and the Three Bears

The bears came home and found Goldilocks.

She went upstairs and fell asleep in baby bear's bed.

Goldilocks tasted the porridge. She ate baby bear's all up.

One day the three bears went for a walk in the woods while their porridge cooled.

Goldilocks opened the door and went into the bears' house.

She sat on baby bear's chair and broke it.

Goldilocks ran away and never came back again.

Three Billy Goats Gruff

- -

At last the Big Billy Goat Gruff came to the bridge. "I'm going to eat you up!" said the Troll. "Come up and try," said the big goat. The Troll did.

- -

Little Billy Goat Gruff went across the bridge. The Troll said, "I will eat you up." "Wait for my big brother," said the little goat. The Troll did.

- -

Big Billy Goat Gruff hit the Troll so hard that he was never seen again.

- -

Now the 3 goats go over the bridge to the hillside to eat grass every day.

- -

Under the bridge lived a bad troll who liked to eat goats.

- -

Once upon a time 3 goats named Gruff wanted to cross a bridge to eat grass on the hillside.

- -

The Second Billy Goat Gruff went across the bridge. "I'm going to eat you up!" said the Troll. "Wait for big brother," said the second goat. The Troll did.

- -

Feed the Pigs

| Pets | Toys | Clothing |

Pigs

Cut these shapes from pink construction paper. Make them as large as your board allows.

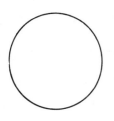

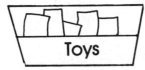

| body | head | snout | ears | feet |

Lay each shape next to the others as you cut so that you can gauge size.

Add details with felt pen.

Pin all parts together on the board.

Add a tail of "curly" pipecleaner.

Troughs

Make construction paper pockets to hold categorizing cards.

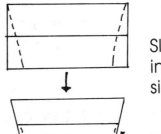

Slant in the sides.

Staple.

Insert a paper clip to allow you to change category headings easily.

Bucket

Hang or set a bucket near the board with the categorizing cards collected together.

 Bulletin Boards That Teach

Pig Bulletin Board

Use this bulletin board for daily practice in categorization.

- Pass out several cards (from the bucket) each day. Children read the cards and place in the correct trough.

- Change categories frequently. Begin with easy differences and work up to fine differences.

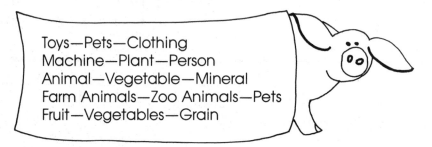

Toys—Pets—Clothing
Machine—Plant—Person
Animal—Vegetable—Mineral
Farm Animals—Zoo Animals—Pets
Fruit—Vegetables—Grain

- Pre-school and kindergarten students may use pictures instead of word cards.

- The board may also be used to build math fact families.

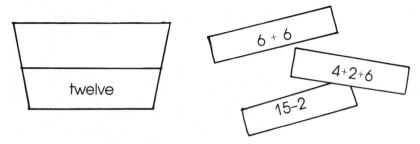

twelve

6 + 6

4+2+6

15–2

- The board works as a free-time activity center.

- Use the cards on p. 47 and 48 as a "starter" set for Pets, Toys and Clothing.

         Bulletin Boards That Teach

 doll

 mittens

 hula hoop

 socks

 wagon

 jacket

 pajamas

 skates

 horse

 hamster

 dog

 guppies

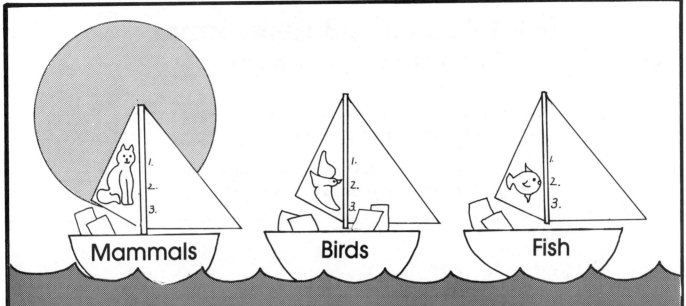

Mammals   Birds   Fish

Put the animals in their boats.

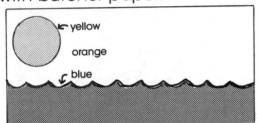

The Ocean

Cover the board with butcher paper.

Make sure this board is in a position where children can reach it to play and practice categorizing.

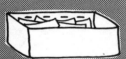

yellow

orange

blue

Sailboats

Boat bottoms are cut from construction paper.

Print the name of the category on the boat with felt pen.

Pin them in place so the top of the boat is open. Children will place the animal cards in here.

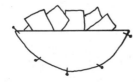

Sails

Reproduce and cut apart the sails provided on pages 50, 51, and 52.

Pin up rulers as masts.

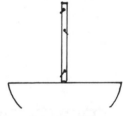

Place sails on either side of the masts.

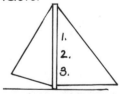

Box and Categorizing Cards

Cover a cardboard box with paper and tack to the board. Place categorizing cards in here.

Animal Families Bulletin Board

Use this board to categorize animal families.

- Make a set of flashcards containing names and/or pictures of birds, mammals and fish.

  - Pass cards out. Child must determine where his card goes, giving the reason for his choice.

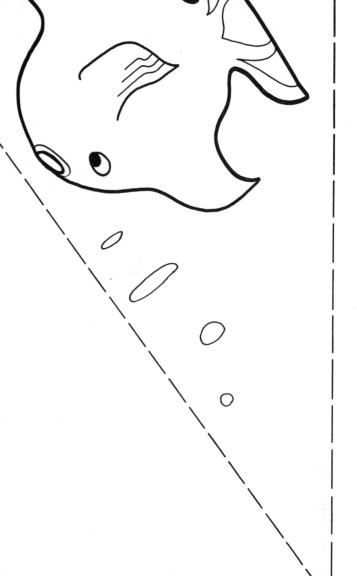

A Fish:

1. breathe with gills

2. move by fins

3. live in water

© by Evan Moor Corporation, 1983

A Mammal :

1. young are fed milk from mother's body

2. most have hair

3. warm-blooded

A Bird:

1. body covered with feathers.

2. young hatch from hard-shelled eggs

3. wings (not all fly)

Count

 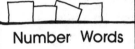 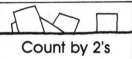 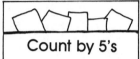

| Ordinals | Number Words | Count by 2's | Count by 5's |

Ten Little Indians

Face

Run 10 copies of the Indian face pattern on page 55. Color or add details with felt pen.

Pin in a row on your board. Make sure it is low enough so that even "small people" can reach it. This bulletin board doubles as a great practice center for students.

Hands

Cut out circles for hands from the pattern page. Pin on the board with 9" x 12" construction paper.

Make a slit in each piece of construction paper and insert a paper clip to allow you to easily slip in different number cards.

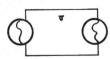

Mocassins

Use brown lunch bags.

Finge top 2" and bend down.

Cut shoe fronts on bottom flap.

Draw center line on moccasins. Pin to bulletin board.

Flashcard Pockets

Display the flashcards that your students need to practice.

Indian Bulletin Board

Use this bulletin board for daily practice in number recognition and number order.

- Provide as many flashcard pockets as you need for the skills you are discussing.

      Numerals to 10
      Ordinal numbers
      Number names
      Counting by 10's, 5's, 2's, etc .
      Counting in another language

- Pass out a set of cards. Children then place them in the Indian boys' hands in the correct order.

- You may begin with number cards already in the hands. Ask a problem or question and have a child select the correct answer.

    Example: How much is 12–5? Child selects 7, etc. . .

- To make practice more challenging, do not always begin with the first number.
  For example:

      Count by 2's   6, 8, 10, etc.
      Count by 5's   25, 30, 35, etc.

- This board may also be used as a free-time activity center.

- On page 56 you will find an activity sheet to use in class or as homework.

Indian Face Pattern for Country Bulletin Board

Color the Kernals of the Maize

red—counting by 5's

orange—counting by 2's

yellow—all other numbers

green—leaves

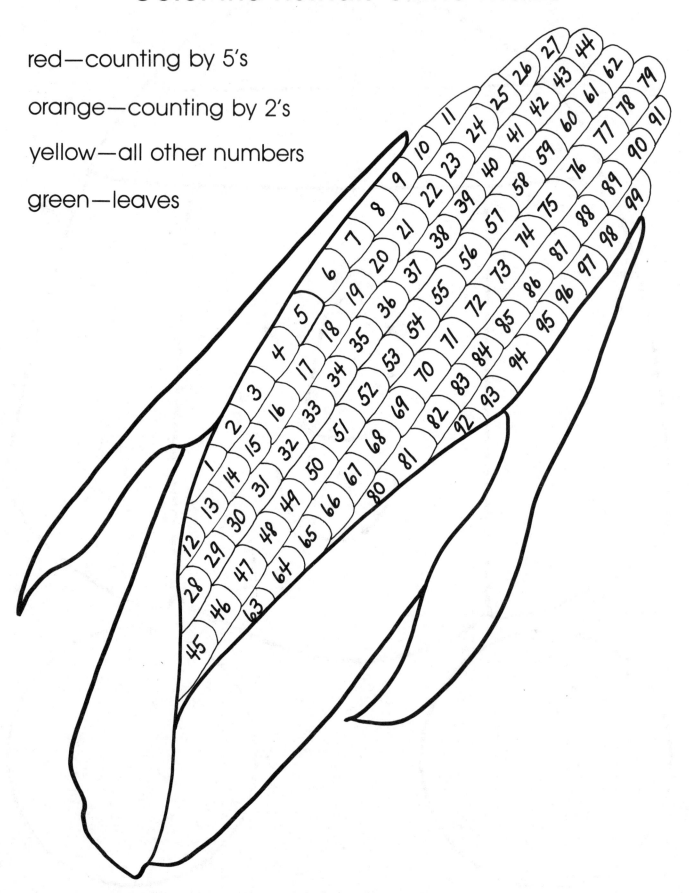

Compound Quiz

Take a peek under my wings.

Flip through and make compound words.

How many did you find?

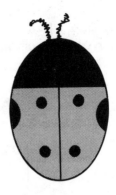

Name
upon   cup
pickle paper
beside top

Score Card
1-10 = Super
5-7 = Good
2-5 = OK
0-2 = Try again!

Ladybug

Use the pattern on page 60 to help you recreate this compound lady bug. Reproduce several of these pages for each bug. Write a different compound word on each sheet. Cut up the dotted line. Mix up word parts to make matching more challenging.

Cut a BLACK oval of construction paper for a base. Cut RED wings the same size as the reproduced compound word sheets. Add black spots.

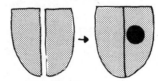

Staple all parts together. Now you can lift the wings separately to match compound word parts.

You can come up with some funny combinations.

Antenna

Use pipe cleaners to create antenna.

Eyes

Glue buttons on for eyes.

Speech Bubbles

Cut out three bubbles. Letter with felt pen.

Score Card

Let students count how many compound words they can find. Put the score card up as a reference for them.

Ladybug Bulletin Board

Use this bulletin board for daily practice in identifying compound words.

- "Thumbs Up"
    One child lifts the ladybug shell. Children put thumbs up if the parts make a compound word and thumbs down if it is not a compound word.

- The "pocket" activities on page 59 may be used as class work or as center activities.

Select compound words suitable for your level.
Include a few "toughies" for a challenge.

airplane	goldfish	oatmeal
applesauce	grandfather	overcoat
	grandmother	
barnyard		pancake
baseball	hailstone	peppermint
bedtime	handbag	pineapple
beside	horseback	
birthday		raincoat
blackbird	inside	rainstorm
buttercup	into	
butterfly		snowflake
	jumprope	streetcar
cameraman		sunshine
chopsticks	ladybug	suppertime
cowboy	lipstick	
crossroad	milkman	upon
cupcake		
		whenever
	nearby	wintertime
dishpan		
drugstore		

Pocket Activities

Make a set of flashcards of compound words. Cut each apart in a different pattern, so the puzzles will be self-checking.

Add an egg timer for children who wish to see how fast they can put the pieces together.

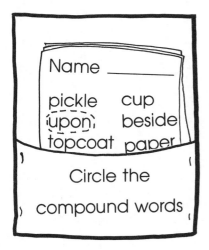

Prepare a worksheet containing words at the reading level of your class. This sheet may be done as a class assignment, center activity, or sent as homework.

Children take paper and fold it into 4 or 8 squares. Using the ladybugs, they write a compound word in each box, then illustrate the word.

       Bulletin Boards That Teach

Ladybug Pattern

60

Bulletin Boards That Teach